I WROTE YOU A LETTER

Marianne Jimenez
I Wrote You a Letter

Isbn: 979-8-89383-822-0

I WROTE YOU A LETTER

MARIANNE JIMENEZ

Thank you to everyone who was a part of this journey. Your presence and patience with me during this time meant the world to me. I went through a difficult time and cursed it for so long, but this experience allowed the most genuine relationships in my life to prosper. I couldn't imagine life without them.

The novel if it were a musical. An anthology of the human design of emotions when we love.

1

Before the End

The Beginning

For I never knew what it was like to be seen
to be heard
A flower forgotten in a garden
slowly dying
I thought I was placed on this earth to always feel like a
stranger
Whittled with the pain of not being heard
but it was with you that I feel familiarity
kindred souls and suddenly every moment before you was
worth the pain
I need you in ways one needs a heart
my heart grows out my body into your soul
blossoming into flowers
a smile that radiates the sun
you'll be my love for eternity
the muse to my poetry
my heart grows the more I love
your unspoken aura is beauty to the world
something so genuine
the love I dreamed of as a little girl
you're a catered rose to my fantasy of love

Spend my Time with Just You

We lay here watching our favorite movie
but is it being watched
because all I see is that face and those tinted lips that kiss me
so well

I love spending time with you
its only you
I feel like the world stops at its feet when I'm with you
it all makes sense when I'm with you
you make me feel so whole

I want to savor this moment
just the two of us in our own world
no one else
no one else is allowed in
its just us two and we do it so well
its been just 5 minutes but somehow the suns gone down

I never want this to change
no I never want this to change
I feel pretty strong when I'm with you
and when we're kissing it feels like my heart is going to
explode
I'm so involve with you
it all just feels so good when I'm with you
and I never want this to change

Impulsive Actions

Ego driven, like a caffeine spur in my system
my chest is risen so high I can touch the roof
the room gets smaller as my ego grows
I'm hearing my impulsive words that spill out like venom
filled with jabs to make you hurt
as drops from your blood fuel my boosting veins with ego
my ego gushes through my veins
a new fresh pump of electricity
the message is sent
I got the last word in this argument
I'm so rushed like a baby bird who just learned how to fly

Last Goodbye

Your finger delicately traces my spine
you feel it's delicacy, so you treat me like a delicate jewel
I hold onto you, in a haven that feels like a safety nest we've
created
our chest are aligned with one another
our heartbeats dance to the drum of our love song
capturing every physical trait of you
I trace 'I love you' on your chest
a token of my love forever tattooed on your heart
looking up, with big wide eyes full of wonder
they meet your beaming smile and flushed cheeks
we look so innocent in this embrace
cherub cheeks and beaming smiles
two angels in an embrace
we danced in the living room that day
naively swaying to a song that foreseen the rest
but in that moment it felt like just us two
caressing every corner there was to be loved
enchanted with our last kiss

I walked out the door and waved goodbye
for what I thought would be moments before I saw you
again
became forever

Repeated Hurt

I'm tired of the same argument
the same words riddled back between us
I don't want to lose you
but I feel like I'm stuck on a carousel
my heart bleeds
my soul crushes
when I'm not near you
but if I stay
it feels like I'm never getting off this carousel
it's spinning me in repetitive loops
There's a voice in my head saying to let go
and I feel like I betray myself every time I ignore that voice
but when I see that face,
the voice is muffled out
fighting to break through

I accept your halfway efforts
I love you with every breath I take
even if it feels like betrayal to accept the love you're only
willing to give

2

The early stages of a breakup

Frenzy

Walking down my favorite street
but it feels like a dream
a dream swerving in
my head is so close to the ground
arriving to the curve and stomping like I got two left feet
one, two, three
counting my steps to feel some structure in my life
I see the world around me through the corner of my eye
but it's silenced by my racing thoughts

The Moon, My Sorrowed Companion

I look up at the moon searching for answers
she stares back at me with a pitiful smile
I know we feel the same
afraid to be the one to break
but it gets us no where
quickly going bad
milk that's been out for too long
and I'm looking at you
and I see that we can't fix it this time

Eat Me, Drink Me

Cursing myself for my impulsive nature
convincing myself I did the right thing
'It had to end'
I repeat to myself a consoling affirmation
but why does it feel like the world is caving in on me
why does my body suddenly feel too big
and awkward for this world
This world has no space for someone that hates every deci-
sion they make
I feel like I just made the biggest mistake of my life
it suddenly feels like a daze
drunken by the whiplash of my decision
dizzy by the pain I feel in my chest
I'm shrinking while the world swallows me whole

Reality Hits in at 8 am

I wake up thinking they'll be a text from you wishing me
good morning
but there's nothing
I almost texted you
but then I remembered were no longer together
we would have talked by now
days are passing by
you're like a ghost
you've vanished and left me behind
I can't seem to find you

Do You Even Know How Much I Love You?

I spoke too soon
I let my emotions rule
now we're not talking
I think I made you mad again
I'm on my tippy toes once again
afraid if I put too much pressure more shells will break
a headache follows me from the pain in my chest
staring at the wall
ignoring your calls
tears stream down to my ears
silence in the room but the subtle vibrations of you trying to
reach me
I wonder how it got so bad
we were so good when did it get so bad
all your insecurities lay heavy on my chest
I carry them but they don't let me breath
their weight controls me and directs me down a path I
don't want
I've got 30 missed calls
you're sending me texts but I hit ignore
I'm struggling to breath
you're on the other side hoping I pick up
pacing your bedroom floor afraid I won't pick up
we're both crying on our bedroom floors
there's no anger in our fight
just two people
afraid to be the one that loves more

Searching for you

I feel I've lost my way
I feel lost in abyss
did I miss a turn
I look at you to guide me through
but I'm just lost in the fog
I search for your blue eyes to guide me through
but they're nowhere in sight
I'm hitting dead ends
I never seem to get you
I think I've lost my way

Music to my soul

I listen to your music just to feel connected
I press play and then you're here
close my eyes and the hums of your voice fill the room
slowly going insane
but that's okay

I try to feel closer to you
your tune is a melody consoling my soul
slowly been going out of mind
I can't lose you
I'll go insane just to keep you around
only then your memory lives on forever
even if you're only in my memory
will dance to your melody
It'll be my only remedy

Say something, show me you care

Feeling like I'm losing you forever
I stare at the raindrops falling down the window
similar to the ones streaming down my cheeks
The laughter left the room with our souls
losing precious time every second we spend apart
time never meant anything to me until I lost you

I wonder if you're holding up
or are you staring out the window wondering as well
Do you want to run out the door and chase after me
and I'll turn back around
run back to you
until our bodies collide
our invisible string tethered together
this time making sure we tie it three times

Back in my dreams

Maybe will never see each other again
maybe this is all done
This ride has finally come to a halt

But is it ever really done
because when I close my eyes
we're back
sitting at our favorite cafe
I'll remember every detail of your face
and the luxury of running my fingers through your soft
strands of hair

Will be swaying like the waves of the ocean next to us
in my dreams we reach every destination at once
our hearts connect again
like two old friends catching up
in my dreams we never broke up
everything is the same
everything makes sense
because in another world we made it work
and when I close my eyes I go to that world

The Warden

Overly conscious of my every move
one wrong move and my house of cards comes tumbling
down

Observing myself
I've got a magnified glass
catching every detail of my every move

my brain is a warden
and my emotions are a prisoner
I have locked the cell for where I keep my heart
not letting any emotion out
silent whimpers
I've put my heart in a lockdown
angry at myself
my own punisher
I will not cry
for I did this to myself
I will not beg
for I can't take another humiliation
I will not scream that I love him at the top of my lungs
even if I feel myself chocking for oxygen
the only release is to scream how much I love him
my lungs are struggling to hold back
gasping for my air
choking with pain
but my mind is a warden that has thrown away the key
and it won't let me say all the things I want to say to you

3

Denial of how special it really was

Turmoil

They say you fight with the one you love
you're screaming
you think I don't care
I'm crying
I think you don't love me
but now we're kissing because we're insane

Swiftly but Leaving an Everlasting Pain

It couldn't have been written in the stars
something so quick and bliss
must've been a bump in the road
must've been a mistake
this couldn't have been meant to be
yet somehow it feels like its destroying me
flipping my world upside down
the moment you left

The Footnote

I stay up late praying the pain away
categorizing you into a lesson
a lesson I needed to learn
taking your value and turning you into a footnote
trying to convince myself you were a topic not a person
because maybe then it'll make sense
why someone I cared for so much is no longer in my life
so if you wonder what you meant to me
I don't have an answer for you
because its so much easier to label you a footnote in my life

You Were Just the First

Maybe will also share the same upbringing
maybe will also both be lefthanded
Just maybe will both squirm in our seat over the same
uncomfortable things
we weren't rare
there are millions of other stories just like ours
you were just the first
they'll be more like you
I'll meet someone who says everything I'm thinking
who reads me like an open book
just the way you did
I'll find another like you

First Other

The leather seats feel cold against my thighs
the interior smell makes me nauseous
his cologne is enough to make me dizzy
Holding back the vile taste in the back of my throat
I stare at him smiling at me
and it feels like he's looking at a corpse with no life behind
her eyes
I fiddle with my rings wishing I could hold your hand and
apologize for what feels like cheating
trying to find oxygen in this tiny space
suffocated by the ego of a man who thinks he's doing every-
thing right

He reaches in for a kiss
I reach for the door
collapsing onto the hard floor
putting as much distance between my mouth and his
running off because I feel like I betrayed us
the harsh wind wipes the tears from my face
I want you to come and save me
hold me tight,
tell me it's okay

but we don't talk anymore
I can't go to you to make me feel safe anymore

3 PART II

I gave it a little more time to when I thought I was ready...

The next three poems are to the boy we meet right after.
Who is sweet and kind and maybe if we had met them first it
would've worked out.

It Was Never You

You've got the sweetest smile
the kindest eyes that look like suns staring down at me
you're the sweetest thing
you've been making me feel better
we've got a routine
you and I

Maybe if I hadn't met him
maybe if he hadn't altered my brain
maybe if my soul didn't feel tied to his
I could love you
maybe

And you hold my hand
carry me when I feel tired
check in on me to make sure I'm okay
we do everything together
a companion
it's so comfortable

But you're not the one
my thoughts still take me back to him
I hate myself for it
you walk by my side and when I turn to look at you
for a second
I hope my eyes meet his
when I hear my phone ring
I hope it's his number I see
the one I've memorized

If Only

I hate to hear you've been crying over me
I know you don't deserve this
you deserve better
someone that genuinely cares
it breaks my heart to see you try so hard to understand
why it's not you
you try for new ways but it gets you no where

If I was smart, I would choose you
it should be you
you're so kind
you treat me so well
you care for me
I know you won't hurt me like he has

I'm hating myself for dragging you along
for being selfish in trying to fill his void
I should forget all about him and focus on us
you should be the one I wake up thinking about
you should be the one I day dream about
and I try to convince myself I can make it work
act affectionate
maybe I'll fool myself too

I'm Not Her

You deserve a better girl
I'm tainted
I'm stuck on him
if we would've met later
throughout a different timeline
in which my heart had time to heal

But I can't see a reality with anyone that's not him
I hate him so much but he's also the only one I've ever loved
I hate that I love everything about him
I love how imperfect he is
I love our passionate love
no one sees us the way we see each other
I can't explain to you how I feel
he would understand what I'm feeling right now

I can't be the person you see yourself with
I know the girl you want me to be
I can't be her
but, you'll just end up resenting me

You deserve someone that loves you
who thinks of you when they walk past a street
who picks up a souvenir from a local shop because they
know you'll love it
who laughs at your jokes
who shares that same warm smile
someone who loves you fully and just you
who only thinks of you

3 PART III

Turtle in a Race

My chest heaves pride
going in to waves
pouring down to my ego
ever so eager to win
If I don't reach the finish line first
what was it worth
I'll have nothing at all
because if you win this race
you'll win once again
collect another medal
meshed from pieces of my heart
so I rather bruise my ankles
because it hurts less than a heart planted on the ground
metal spikes hitting glass floor
if I let you win this
you'll win and take everything once again
and I'll be left with nothing
once again

Dark Stickiness

A sorcery
a darkened night
covering my youthful soul
the sun doesn't shine anymore
covered by the dark sky

I'm not who I once was
I'm a fevered poison
a dark shadow that once shined in the light

Walking past people that see the same girl
but when I look in the reflection
I see the reflection of a girl who died
and now I'm forced to carry her body

In a maze
I can't find a way out of
there's no exit sign
just a new corner deceiving itself as a way out
fooling me again
and again
riddled with shame
for I can't bring myself out
nothing I say feels genuine
I'm so lost in this maze of thorns and lies
I can't rouse myself from the nightmare that follows me

Caution Ahead: Rough Road

I guess I just really feel alone
walking around with no backpack
there's no map in my hands
or directions to guide me home
a tornado took me in
swirling me relentlessly
ungrounding me from everything I know

Then it spit me back out
like I never mattered
no hint of remorse
it sent me to a place I never been
dark and lonely
abandoned with no form of getting back home
unaware if that home still exists
I'm alone with no direction

Full Room, Empty Heart

I try to tell myself its okay to be alone
convince myself I still have time
but everything I do feels wrong
being alone feels like losing
I must've done something wrong

They say being alone doesn't mean you're lonely
yet I'm surrounded by people that know me
while sitting in a corner with warm lights
but there's a coldness in my chest
for the one person I want is nowhere near this room

4

Melancholic Heartbreak

When the dust finally settles. When all the denial ends, and you realize that you lost someone you cared for. And everything just feels dark. The light that they brought into your life seems as it is gone.

Pull and Tear

Between us I'll admit
we threw in the towel
at the tip of the iceberg
we never reached it
so much love waiting to be teared into the world
like a child coming out the womb,
waiting to let out its first cry
yearning to be seen

A love desperate to stay
we covered it up
buried it six feet underground as it tried to kick up for air
our love is buried
here and there I still see the soil underneath move
a love fighting to be heard
it'll come out the grave the second we tried to dig it out
run back straight into our chests

Needle and a Thread

Our love is gone
but she was desperate to leave a mark
so she sowed herself into our chests
always a mark
visible only to us
a haunted shadow following us
a broken thread poking out our chest
a thin needle sticking out
silently reminding us with trickled pain that she existed

My Love for You Consumes Me

I love you so much
I wish I could vomit those words out to you
you consume my every thought
I fall asleep happily knowing you'll be in my dreams

I love
love you

I'll love you all the time
in every moment
in everything I do
I'll express my love to you

Come Back Please

I hold you close my chest
like a delicate flower that's been withered
I try to protect it but is there any fight left in it

I guess I still hope you'll come back
the door will open and I'll see my lover
time will trace back and you'll still be holding me
telling me it was all a mistake
you'll go back to being my protector
take back all the hurt
go back to when you once cared
and guarded my feelings

White Car

Staring at the streets your tires once marked
hoping I'll see that white ford pull up again
people drive up this street everyday unaware of its history
sometimes I look out and see a white car
and hope each time
I'll see that dainty boy with a lopsided smile come out the car
I hope I'll see that smile that's so imperfect but perfect to me
those eyebrows that curve to the shape of your eyes
I say I'm fine but sometimes I wish I could camp on that
sidewalk
hoping I'll catch a glimpse of your car one day

My Heart is Set on You

I can't renounce my love for you
I pray every night you'll come back
I break my heart turning it into a shattered mess
waiting to hear from you

Love means nothing if it's not with you
spring comes around and I don't feel the sun shining down
on me
the only warmth I feel is when I lay next to you
after everything I refuse to give up

Hold On, I Still Had So Much Love to Give You

I would've loved you forever
but now it's all gone
like dust in the wind
my love for you was real
it was real

You'll never know something real
my love reaches depths deeper than the ocean
new layers to unfold the deeper it goes

I cry for you
my puddle of tears fill the bathtub I'm in
baby my love was pure
wanted to hold you close
baby all I wanted was you
all I wanted was us
but now it's all gone
oh but I still love you

All Do Anything Just to Have You Back

I'll give you the key to my heart
hope you care enough to come back
wishing on a star that you won't forget about me
you'll remember that girl you once knew
come back to me and unlock my heart
I hope you care to not leave it in the dark
I'll lay out my cards just for you
hope you care to come back

I Saw You in a Stranger's Face

I saw someone that looked like you
I was at the grocery store
I still remember the smell of the aisle I was on
gripped onto a shelf
holding myself up
it hit me like a painful slap to the face
I gasped for air
but the grocery store was closing in on me
I stare at him for answers to questions I've held for months
but as we make eye contact
I realize he doesn't have them
he's just a stranger watching another stranger
unfold in front of them

How it Felt to Have You for Just a Glimpse

I saw that stranger that looked just like you
and I felt the emotions hit me like a wave
that wave took me whole and drowned me
I was slowly
painfully flooded with every memory
the wave took me through the depth of my emotions
a film that's been processed ready to show every memory its
captured

Paddling my arms and feet trying to catch a breath
consumed with painful nostalgia
my arms held me up
fighting the gravity pulling me down

Down to the floor where I would sob
mesh with the cement in a puddle of tears
use the glue of my tears to attach my heart to the ground
in that moment I could flood the grocery store as my tears
would ricochet
one after the other
because for just a moment I thought I had you once again

I Keep Falling for You

My heart yearns for your touch
a melody plays in my mind from your piano tunes
to feel your long, rough
but soft fingers interwind with my own
sometimes when I think I'm over it I seem to fall back
like trying to get off a merry go around
never successfully getting up without falling back down
my heart remembers you more than my mind
I'm reaching out for a ghost
when I reach for your memory it fades away
leaving only the smoke of your afternoon cigarette

Every Map Leads to You

I've molded into a different person
but my heart stays that same
my maps always lead me to you
you're always my final destination

Through it all
you're the only one my heart recognizes
it's like the same old road you take driving back home
the same coffee order you get every morning

The stars in my eyes draw out a constellation
the constellation is a map leading me back home
my soul only feels at home when its near you

Do your roadmaps lead you back to me
do the stars in your eyes draw out the constellation to my
smile

You Don't Know How Much I Really Care

I care for you deeply
I wake up with a bitter taste in my mouth
my days seem so gloomy
I'm decaying internally
I pray every morning today is the day you'll come save me

Be The Only One

I want you to be the only one
the only one that completes me
the only one I dream of
the only one burned inside my thoughts
the only one I long for
the only one I care for at the end of the day
please be the only one

Twin Flame

I hope we collide
I hope we find the perfect stillness in the tide
clash into each other and create a perfect kaleidoscope

Fuse our souls together
coming in like one flame
two separate flames coming back as one
I hope one day we collide
and create a fire from the match of our love

Melancholy emptiness

A stranger who's seen me
a stranger who has held me when I cried
a stranger I laid with an aligned heartbeat
a stranger I have memories with

I keep our memories in a book
I've shoved that book to a corner to collect dust
it hurts too much to keep the book in sight
sometimes I revisit that book
I glare at the pages that hold memories we once lived
was it real if I struggle to remember how it was
what once felt like forever is gone just like you

Misery is When I Miss My Baby

I try to be a strong soldier
try to be the toughest I can be and not cry
but as I tilt my head back to stop the tears
I shut my eyes and see your face
and one by one the tears stream down my face
past my ears and onto the floor
watering a garden full of my own pain
flowers have blossomed
but they're hidden by thorns and vines
a beautiful rose lies there hidden
engulfed by the painful thorns that don't let it breath

The Things You'll Never Know

You'll never know why I hate peanut butter with chocolate
or how I hate big crowds
how my heart feels like it's exploding when I'm near you
because of how much I really like you
you'll never know how funny I am
how I scrunch my nose when I lie

Mostly,

You'll never know how lucky you are to be loved by me
I would've shown you the love you never had
because I loved everything about you
I loved your soul and who you were
they won't feel the soul tying devotion I did
I express my love through figurative phrases
I could've written you thousands of endless love poems
but now I'm left to write you heartbreak doodles

Almost Happily Ever After

You've got a stubborn mind
can't see what it's like to have it all
maybe if you knew
you could've known
how lucky we were to have found this love so young

But you rather just leave
than to fight for true love
you lose before you even try
play a track you've memorized
it's safer to follow the path you know so well
because you fear what you don't understand

It's a shame to watch you throw us away
throw what we had like rotten trash
so much life in it that you could've nurtured
just like every good thing in your life
you toss it away before giving it a chance

It'll just pass you by
good things will always pass you by
and you'll never know
you'll never know a good thing when you have it

Your Words Feel like Knives but I Still Love you

You said I was safe with you
but I was the one always holding your hand
you loved spinning me around
unaware of how sick you were making me
convincing me of love that was not there

It makes me sad
it was real on my end
I was so devoted to you
I trusted you endlessly

even when you said 19 was too young
while we laid naked in your bed
I was just 19
you made me hate my age
blame myself for being younger than you
but I wanted to believe we were real
because it was for me

What Can I Do to Make You Want Me Again

I can show you how much you mean to me in different ways
to see which one will make you stay
which one makes you want to try again
I'll shape shift into whatever you want me to be
as long as you stay

4 PART II

Contact with your ex

Finally

I can't believe it
we're finally back
six months have passed and we're finally talking again
pick up the phone
easy conversation like nothing's happened
I'm so anxious to get us back to where we once were
I've got my baby back
the world is back in technicolor
I'm finally back at the pace of the world

I Wait

I sit in silence
it's been a few hours since I've heard from you
I sit by my phone
longing for a response
those hours become into days
but I sit
frozen in time until I hear from you again
I'm so confused
why are you so busy
you used to respond in seconds
why can't it be just like that

Now I wait
wait until you want me again
and decide I'm worth responding to

Crumbs

I see your name on my screen
that beautiful name across my screen
my heart skips a beat with excitement enough to overrun the
quiet feeling of dread in my stomach

I take the crumbs you give me
if that means I get some of you
I hope after this you won't leave me on read again
I hope I won't lay awake at night hoping you'll respond

But quickly after that call you're back to no response
it feels like a sick game that you hold control of
the headmaster
you're calling all the shots
you must really like this

Is this how it feels to not be cared by you
to be treated like a rag that you throw to the side
I turn off my phone
hoping I'll see your name when I turn it on
I try to go to bed but my body is shaking with nerves
I'm letting you bring me to an episode
but maybe it'll be worth it if I get to have you again

It's Okay I Can Take the Pain

You've hurt me once again
thought I'll be used to the pain
but it all just hurts the same
I hold you in high regards
or is it my everlasting hope that you'll be different
I always hope you'll see my pain
you'll see how it hurts
you'll care
but you treat me like a ghost
a page you've turned
shoes you outgrew
so you step all over me with your new shoes

I guess I do it to myself
if you don't care
I guest I hurt myself
I give you my energy
constantly filling your belly
you suck me dry
leave me with nothing
but a huddled mess
picking up the pieces
picking up what's left of me
because you leave me feeling so empty
so regretful
and I'm back to square one
wondering why I ever gave you my energy

Be My Friend

If we can't be lovers again
I hope we can be friends
it's all I ever wanted
for us to be friends
because even just a piece of your heart is enough

Trying to Keep it Cool

Five things you can see
four things you can touch
three things you can hear
two things you can smell
one thing you can taste

I repeat 5 times a day
have me in a mess
I'm fighting panic attacks
have I been longing for a ghost that no longer exists
have I been chasing a love that clearly died

Please Don't Let me be Wrong About You

Is there someone else
is there someone who's getting your full attention while
I beg
is there someone who gets graced with your presence
while I'm left imagining how you look
is that why you wake up at 3 am to text me back

Please, please, please,
allow me the decency of a peaceful death
don't tell me you're stringing me along when you've found
somebody else

Fighting For Us

The people that love me hate you
they see me deteriorate and they hate that I let you back in
they see you smothering me
but I'm so willing to protect you against everyone protecting
me

They don't know you
they don't know us
if they did they'll understand
why I fight so hard
why I don't let go of the tethered rope causing me burns

They tell me I deserve better
but it sounds like harmful attacks to our love
tell me I'm better than this but I can't accept anything
without you in it

4 PART III

Heartbreak that keeps on giving

Cure For Love

Harsh white lights of a hospital room
equipment picking up my fragile state
my body gave in
I did everything
there's nothing left for me to give
doctors and nurses trying to find the reason for my sickness
why I don't eat
why I vomit every morning
they don't understand this odd disease
I have the answer for their mystery
I'm sick from love
I'm sick from you
the cure to it all is to forget you
but I know there's no such cure
so I let them look through their notes
scrummage to find reasoning for the mystery that's you

Cold Hard Truth

I lay on the cold hard floor
my bed feels unsafe
the sheets feel like a foreign cloth on my skin
it makes my skin crawl
I feel safe against the cold hard floor
so I sleep on the floor
praying to have the pain removed from my broken mind

Crying
I feel like a kid
I wish my mommy was here to hold me
I can't be a human right now
the responsibilities of being a person are buried by the heart-
break I feel

I Can't Pretend Anymore

My alarm rings
like a painful reminder that I have to pretend everything's
okay
but I can't
the warrior in me has been my demise
there's no fight left in me
so I ignore the alarms
I miss class
I miss work
I can't bring myself to get up
I can't bring myself to show up
I can't bring myself to eat
I wake up nauseous from the heartbreak
my body rejecting the pain that you've caused

Down

I can't go lower than this
it doesn't get worse than this
this is it
if I can survive this
I can survive anything

Ashes to (Ash)es

I fought with my love and soul
and came back with nothing in return but a body
haunting my room like a ghost
standing like a soldier with an empty stare
who's come back from war but lost everything
my mind stayed in the battlefield
I feel like nothing but ash
I'm back as just a distorted glimpse of who I was

I Hate Your Memory

Your memory stays
it's haunts me now
a torturous reminder of what once was
and never will be again
day and night it haunts me now
I hate myself
I hate ever letting you in
because now your memory taints my broken heart
it's buried deep in my head

Betrayal Killed it All

The betrayal was what hurt the most
because now we're really done
there's no going back
I could never look at you the same
I could never trust you again
you ruined the last hope
I can never forgive you for killing my hope

I Cared; I Was the Only One

I fell into it deeply
you knew it and you loved it
I gave you my love and kissed all your scars away
I ruined myself just for you
you took the fire from me
took it and left me with nothing
left me hurting inside
triggered me into an episode
you never really cared for me
you don't shatter the hearts of people you love

Hope For Love Died

Feels like I'm dying
it feel like absolute death
when the person you love kills all hope of love

I feel so let down
how could you share what we had with somebody else
bringing to the surface all my insecurities I didn't know
I had
you left me with a broken heart
with broken hope of all we could've been
because I know it's all gone now
we will never be one again
we're all over now
I can see that now

Why Me, Not You?

Can you tell me how to move on
you make it look so easy
you flipped the page so quick
the wake up was so cruel
that's your expertise
you terrify me now

Why can't you hurt the way I hurt
why is it me who hurts all the time
why is it you thrive
when I'm dying, crying
why is it me and not you

Enjoy Your Privilege

You said I was the only one for you
was I so wrong to believe
I don't trust easily but I trusted you
how could you be so cruel

Cradled up in bed
wishing I never met you
wishing our eyes never met
wishing I could turn back time and quit that job earlier
An unaware victim
walking into your trap
I would've been better off
because nothing hurts more than loving someone that
doesn't love you anymore
enjoy the privilege of not knowing what it's like to be
betrayed by someone you love

Never Would've Done That to You

I wish you cared for my feelings
I know you don't owe me anything
but I wish it could've been the last promise you kept
I wish it could've been your last act of love
I wish you didn't get with someone that likes to rub it in
that paints a picture perfect image
whether it's real or not it's feels like death by a thousand cuts
I wish you would've cared of how it made me feel
I would've

Hero becomes the Villain

Everything about you breaks my heart
it makes my stomach turn
and I feel that acid build up
it's coming out ready to spill the lies and betrayals my body
holds against you
it's like you find a new way to hurt me each time
I feel alone and depressed
the one person I want to make me smile is killing me
you have all this power over me
and you control it so well
my fragile heart that you tore apart with your teeth
spit out lies through your gritted teeth
You've become a monster
you're my walking nightmare
I feel a cold shiver run down my spine when I hear
your name
you cause me so much pain
when will you show me mercy and stop hurting me
this much

Story of My Pain

I don't know how to tell you how I feel
so I'll rhyme it out
to let you know the ways in which you've killed me
but my words deceive you
these pretty words that I write
you think it's alright
you think I'm in love but I'm hating you

And I'm always crying
I hate my puffy eyes
one more salty tear dedicated to you
so I'll take what's killing me and turn it into flowers
and my left hand shakes as I write with pain
unfolding this story on a piece of paper filled with tears

__I Wish We Never Met (truly)__

With experiences come lessons that you learn
at most this heartbreak brought me wisdom
I know I'm supposed to see it that way
tell myself that loving someone is never a waste
but deep down to the very depth of my heart
I wish we never met
if there was a machine that could erase you from my
memory
I would spend my life's earnings paying whatever it cost to
erase you from my mind
erase every moment
laugh
touch

I know we're supposed to take these experiences and apply
them as learning experiences
but when I say,
'I wish I could erase your existence from my mind'
I mean it with every fiber of my body

5

The Anger Stage

Evil Thoughts of You

I said I would always love you but I curse you now
I guess you can call me a liar
maybe my love wasn't as unconditional as I thought
it would be a lie if I said I wished you well

I know it's not your fault
I know it's not your fault that it hurt me so much
I know you did it for yourself
but doing it for yourself slammed me to the ground

My world cascades around me
I struggle to find air
you crushed my lungs
destroyed me from the inside out
and left me in broken pieces
I struggle to find air consumed with the dust of what you
broke
coughing up pain and trauma from my memories
you said you did this for yourself
but you killed me along the way
you saved yourself while holding my head under water

The Boy is Mine

I hate her
I hate every little thing about her
I hate her with such a rage you would think I know her
but I don't know her
she's just a stranger I hate
hate her for taking what's mine
showing off my belongings like they're hers
trying on shoes that don't fit her
she's taken my chair
I hate her for intruding my home
she doesn't know its previous owner
she loves second hand clothing
willing to take without knowing its owner
guess that's what happens when you give it away
she smiles so bright wearing my clothes
my shoes fit her too big
so she stuffs socks in hoping no one will notice
she's got what she's wanted
flashing a big smile in front of the mirror
head to toe disguised as good
but really just a villain hidden behind the mask
she mimics my posture
hoping the clothes will help her reach me
she's not me but she sure plays the part
I hate this stranger for taking what's mine showing it off like
it's hers
but the tags on the clothes say my name

She's Not Me

She's not me
why'd you stoop so low
were you really that lonely
you know she'll never get you

Baby you look so dead
you look so dead when you're around her
she won't bring you life the way I did
I know you feel my absence
anytime you try to love on her
baby she'll never know you how I did
she won't undress the very depth of your mind

Hate You for Proving Them Right

I want to scream at the top of my lungs

I fucking hate you
I fucking hate you

Because how could you
every promise you made
you snapped it in my face
I try to be nice
try to show love
wish you the best but I really don't
I really don't
because I fucking hate you
and I'm not wrong
I'm not wrong

Everybody hates you
I see it now
I had your back
against them all
I had your back when you took the knife to my back
you made me look like a fool
you made them right
every warning
they were right
oh they were right

Glue Gun With broken Glass

All the issues that you had I thought I could fix them
I thought I could be there for you unconditionally
the way your daddy never was
show you loyalty the way your mommy never did
show you love can be kind and gentle
have our love be different from the one you grew up with
show you betrayal doesn't come with love

But instead
you showed me what haunts you
you showed me what you view love as
I thought my love was enough
but nothing is ever enough for you

Unknown Artist

Said you wanted to be an artist
yet always embarrassed of the music you made
I guess that's why you sample music now
said you took up producing
don't you need an artist for that
baby give it up and take that 9-5

I See You

We took a break to figure ourselves out
chase our dreams
time has passed
I was the only that stuck to the plan
my dreams attained a physical form
I finally began writing again
got new hobbies
but you stayed the same
you stuck to what you knew
found someone to fill the void
cover the fact that you'll never do anything for yourself
avoid the insecurity that you'll never be someone
but I see it now
I see you for what you are
so live knowing there's someone else in this world who
knows how miserable and pathetic you really are

I Just Hate it All

I'm so angry
so disappointed
in you
in myself
in this whole mess
I say I hate you
but I know it's because I still feel so much
I've never felt betrayal
I don't know what to do with all these negative emotions
I guess hate and love truly are similar

I hate that you ruined it for me
I hate that I can't go back to when I once felt so fond of you
I hate that there's a negative cloud around you
I hate that you made me hate you

Confusing Emotions

Because I say I hate you
but I would run back to you if you called
I would tell you how much I love you
because I try and I try
but I could never hate you

My tears did they wash over the promises
because your gone
and holding someone new
I hate to think I didn't matter to you
did you forget me that easily

I hold you close to my chest
you hurt me countless times
you don't know it hurts me
would you even care

Body Rejects You

Mind games pouring down my soul
convincing me I was safe with you but you've brought me so
much pain

And I always felt like shit around you
you always brought down all my dreams
play pretend you were an arson in my bedroom
I could never trust you
always poking at me
my body used to shake in nervousness whenever I came
near you
I could never fall asleep lying next to you

Tit for Tat

I want you to feel knots in your stomach
the way I did
I want you to stay up late at night tossing
the way I stayed up for you

I want you to look at your phone waiting for a text that
won't come through
I want you to ponder every moment
I want you to blame yourself
even when you did nothing wrong
I want you to rock yourself to sleep with tears streaming
down your eyes
I want you to feel what I did
when you tore out my heart

I want you to feel what I felt
every second of it
does that make me bitter
oh well
I want you to pray the pain away
hope you never met them

Because you're so happy
pretending you didn't kill me
pretending you didn't ruin me
because you never talk about it

You're Not the Good Guy

You get to be the good God almighty
pretend I didn't exist
wipe your hands clean of the crime
pretend there's not a girl out there you completely destroyed
wiped her innocence away and destroyed her concept of love
that's what angers me the most
that you get to pretend you didn't kill me
get your happy ending
while I sit holding my tongue
covering wounds that keep on bleeding
when I just want to scream to the world that you're not the
person you pretend to be
you're not this kind person you convince others you are
tell them how truly vile you are
I'm tired of covering your crime
I'm tired of protecting you

6

The war is over. Yet, everything just feels still and lonely.

~depression doodles~

Why?

Why do the good things die so quick
why did we end so quick
was it ever meant to be
were we ever meant to be
were you ever for me
would've sworn I had known you my whole life

Sometimes There is No Rainbow

I'm tired of hearing there's a rainbow after the storm
or for there to be flowers there needs to be rain
I wish I didn't know this pain
I wish I didn't know a person could cry this much
I wish I was oblivious to this pain
I wish I didn't know
because the rain is flooding
and there's no bloom

And I Wonder

Sometimes I wonder why things had to change so much
I'm different
you're different
everything's changed
nothings the same even if we tried
we're not those kids who once fell in love
those kids don't exist anymore
I look at you and see a stranger
I don't see that boy I used to know
that crooked smile doesn't hold warmth
your slightly sloppy left eye isn't cute but asymmetrical
your quirky features don't make my soul smile anymore but
are simple observations
with time we buried those kids who once fell in love with
each other

We used to talk for hours but now we don't talk at all
I used any excuse to hear you talk because your voice
sounded like angels singing my favorite song
but now it sends piercing blades straight to my chest
what you said used to matter to me so much
you were an accolade to me
I hate to wonder if it was ever real
or was it heightened by my emotions towards you

Was it Real?

Was the love real
did we both we feel it
did you heart beat for me the way mine beat for you
did the hurt puncture your heart ripping it into a million
pieces
and do you find yourself still picking up pieces that seem so
scattered
because I do

How did we get so far from each other
if the love was real why are we strangers now
you know I think of when we were together
I wonder what happened
we were so close
so close to it all
but now we're just strangers
I look at you and see nothing
I don't recognize you
you're not that boy I once fell in love with

You're Where I Go When I Want to Feel Depression

I look at you in disgust
you're a morbid gush of darkness
and to know you is tainting
latching onto your darkness pretending it's mine too
your memory is like a shadow that reminds me of the fight to
pull myself out the dark
detach myself from your strings of darkness
because to be near you is just dark

Strange Things

It's strange
how it all comes and goes
it comes like a shifting wind so unexpected
unexpectedly but then you can't imagine life before it
how did I live without knowing this feeling
how did I live without knowing my days could feel this
bright

Isn't it strange how life changes in a moment
A naïve soul
given sweet fruit
but it's all borrowed
those sweet moments that feel like forever
seem to always be borrowed
what once was is now just a memory

Isn't it strange how something so real eventually fades into a
memory
they say nothing good can ever last
but I fade into the mistake it'll last this time
and as I'm about to grab it
it disappears
leaving a bitter taste in my mouth
shifting my world and forever changing me

I see the ghost of who I was when it all made sense
when it felt like everything was perfect
my ghost dances in my memory

what a wicked thing
to know the feeling of happiness and have it wiped away
left as just a memory
a far away feeling

Skipping Steps

I form the pieces to a new map
always willing to resort
but every time I think I've found my way I miss a step
that step makes me fall into a deep hole
ungrounding me from what I know
that step is so cruel
they convince me they're someone that they're not
they pretend to feel safe
providing me fake cushion ready to be removed at any
moment
that step seems so real but it's all just so fake
because they never care
just ready to make me fall
the fantasy of it all
seems so thrilling to them all
Make a girl fall over a fake step
because he and many like him
are just steps
fake steps to make you trip
question what you know
pretend to be secure
but the stomach drop when you fall
feels like whip lash to harsh reality
the truth is out
you were a decoy set to make me fall
I've learned to skip a step instead of skipping a beat
my heart skips no beats for a decoy
you're just a step to be skipped

La Ola Violenta
(Spanish poem)

Y sí cuando te vuelvo aver ciento el malestar en mi barriga
lo sentiré en ese momento que esto nunca se va ser
porqué eres cómo la marea

Desconectándome y tomándome entera ya no tengo control
nado en tu mar
en tu mar de errores
en tu mar de dolor
en tu mar de confusión
desorientada tratando de regresar atrás a la cubierta

Tu me desvías
sin conoce me desalojo
porqué detrás de cada momento juntos hay dos de dolor
sufrí como sí nunca avía sentido dolor
me causa regresar a fragmentos de cuando me hicisteis caer
ya no somos los que antes fuimos
ya no te amo
no supiestes cuidar mi corazón
no te importó
lo dejastes ir con la marea
el dolor que me causastes seguirà por los anos
y si al verte siento ese malestar en mi barriga sé correr en la
dirección contraria.

Oizys

She's so unpredictable
I never know what she's going to take next
sometimes I'm happy and my laughter wakes her up from
her slumber
and she's back up to ruin my life
Oizys sometimes feels comforting but it's because she makes
the walls feel like they're caving in on me
I fight with Oizys everyday
why has she chosen me as a victim
she consumes me and makes me feel lost
she tears up my dreams living me in somber state
her only goal is to ruin me
she's so good at what she does
I had to give her a name
I've known her for too many years
it seems she enjoys the home she's built in my mind
I never truly defeat her before she's back up again
Oizys she's like a poison in my mind
she's the depression that latches onto my back

Numbing Cream

I rarely feel anything
moments just pass me by
fleeting moments I try to catch up
but nothing ever makes sense or feels real to me
I chase you through an empty field
promise you whatever it takes for your attention
yet we both know I'll leave once I have it
I always leave
it's just what I do
what I do all the time

Actor Playing His Part

He smelled like roses
he smiled like an angel
I thought he could never hurt me
but he held the knife behind his back
and when he held me I didn't feel the way he was silently
killing me
he was making me bleed
but his smile was so blinding
I thought he was fixing me

You're so tricky
always pretending
you play your part so well
I was just an act in your play
a simple act in your play
you turn around to face the camera
and tell everyone how you played me so well

Beauty In Pain

I write the best when my life's falling apart
my tears meet with the ink on my pen
smudging what's left of this pain
I write the best when I'm depressed
the most beautiful heart wrenching words
guess it's all beauty in the end

Why You?

The worst part of all this is the betrayal
what did I do to deserve this
I don't consider myself to be the worst person
what did I do to hurt like this
all I did was fall for you
why did you have to hurt me like this
why did our paths align
I'll always ask myself
I'll always ask why you
why did I fall for someone so cruel
someone who didn't value the love I gave them
who didn't care that I trusted them with my feelings
dismissed my attempt to fight for us
all I wanted was to care for you
and I just might always ask myself
what I did to deserve someone like you

Story Repeats

Sometimes I cry
I cry for that little girl
she only ever wanted that fairytale love
she thought love was kind and gentle
she thought you would treat her right

I trusted you
I free fell into your arms
I really thought you were the one
I was happy
every pain and thorn in the past was worth it
they all led me to you
all the mistakes I had made
vanished when I was next to you
but when you left
you made me feel like baggage
I was once again that little girl begging her dad to care for her

To my family, friends, and therapist Connie. Whose words left an everlasting impression on me during this chapter of my life. Your words were exactly what I needed to hear at the time.

"We don't own people, even when you date them no one is ever yours people are borrowed." – J.J

"We don't own people, even when you date them no one is ever yours people are borrowed." – J.J

"There was someone before them, they'll be someone after them." – J.J

"There was someone before them, they'll be someone after them." – J.J

"It's heartbreaking to see, he didn't just lose you but you both lost each other." - N.V

"You're too pretty to be sad over a guy, if he doesn't see what he lost, HIS LOSS." – J.M

"What he does has nothing to do with you." C.T

"You can't avoid heartbreak just because you chose not to love. Heartbreak is everywhere. One day someone you care for dies and that's heartbreak. So, love. Love hard and love deeply because heartbreak is inevitable." – C.T

"We don't get a crystal ball that tells us how everything plays out. We simply don't know so just let it be." – C.T

"Y no se te olvide mi niña, del amor nadie se muere." – N.V

7

The final stage of a heartbreak: We move on through self-reflection.

Protecting My Kingdom

I'm like a kid throwing a tantrum
I kick my feet because it doesn't go my way
I say things harshly and rash
hoping to get the upper hand
but I'm just hurting you
hurting myself by ruining something I care for
I act impulsive to protect myself
I somehow fear my vulnerability is a weakness
to gain control I act impulsively
I destroy
I burn towers
my wicked tongue fumes out fire

Self-Awareness

I aim for perfection
I feel so imperfect but if I do a good job at pretending
maybe just then
I can convince myself I'm perfect

If I look in the mirror I see my own enemy
I hold myself to the highest standard
don't allow myself to be human
no one would believe how insecure I really am
I carry myself so well
but I struggle to show kindness to myself
I've been untouchable my whole life
allowed no one to teach me anything
I've had it figured it out since I was young
never needed no one but myself

I need to be perfect
if I'm the only one I can count on
but it's so exhausting
I know I'm wrong
I know I need to be kinder to myself
but it's like reprogramming my mind
retraining it from its innate state
I'm still learning
but I want to change
because I see it only hurts me
I'll reprogram my mind
baby steps to being human
and maybe tomorrow I can be a little kinder to myself

Started As a Kid

I hate waiting for people to do things for me
I hate when people have access to hurt me
so I taught myself how to ride a bike
slammed into walls
fell and scraped my legs until I learned
learned how to read
read small one-sentence books every night
until I reached books with full sentences
I shut myself out from my family so that no one could
hurt me
the quiet child in the corner who always did everything
herself
the daughter that never needed help from her parents
she had it figured it out

I put myself in safety mode at a very young age
quickly saw how hurtful it was to depend on people
give them a chance to hurt you
I didn't want to give that power to anybody
but it made me very lonely
I learned everything but how to communicate my feelings
I don't know how to ask for help
I'm a tough soldier
I'm independent but I feel lonely
and I wonder if I'll ever let people in

I Got Through It

I got through the toughest hill
a battle I was starting to fear I would not survive
for just a second
I thought this was the thing that would destroy me
I waved a white flag but it was ignored
I paddled my arms and feet trying to go up shore
but I was swallowed by the waves
drowning and screaming for help but no one around

Stuck in quicksand
but I pulled myself out
I somehow did it
I channeled the fire deep in my belly
and pulled myself out
I rewired everything I knew and shed my old skin
I got through it
it didn't kill me
I did the toughest thing known to mankind
and faced my own self

For the Teddy Bear Hearts

I used to think being emotional was a weakness
to let things affect you so deeply was shameful
life moves on and so should you
never take things too seriously
but it takes courage to be emotional
to not sweep feelings under the rug
to confront them face to face
to allow yourself to admit when something hurt

I feel things so deeply
I get hurt easily
but I also love so deeply
I feel every feeling there is to be felt
I make my pain into art
when I'm happy I feel ecstatic
when I'm sad I feel wounded
but I feel
and I feel deeply
there is strength in feeling your emotions proudly
it is not a weakness to be sensitive
but unfound
undiscovered
strength

New Self

The sun's been hidden for months
but I went outside today
the sun was shining down on me again
I felt the warm waves radiate a glow throughout my skin
feeding me back to life
I feel the warm sun on my skin again
I hear my genuine laughter again
I've ran into myself once again

It's been a while
I look different
I look wiser
more gentle
more aware
more present
I know what I want
I keep myself grounded in situations that try to shake me
I prioritize myself
I know my threshold
when to recharge before I reach red
I'm back to myself but in a different way

I like this version
she's in her energy
no need to impress
silently making herself through the crowd
her silent aura flows in magnetic waves
I like this version of myself
she's finally out the woods

Gratitude

There's a certain electricity that flows through you after
being in the dark for so long
you value the small things
learn to never take the small victories for granted again

I am present
I inhale the salty smell of the waves as I walk through the
grainy hot sand
the way my toes interlace with a sprig of grass as I walk
through a field
the way I am able to touch a textured rock and feel it's
history through my palms
the warm embrace of someone's else chest against my own
the excitement in someone's eyes when they tell me news
the smile across someone's face as they wave at me
I came out the dark tunnel and into the light

I value every moment
present gratitude to the simplest gestures of life
I am present
I am grateful
I am here now

Thank You to Friends

I've met the kindest souls on this journey
when I fell they picked me up
laughter echoed through the rooms as we laughed
they untied the knots in my chest
wiped the tears streaming down my face
walked with me when the road got lonely
showed me that life doesn't end when someone breaks your
heart
picked up the pieces they didn't break
and sowed them back up tenderly with roses
gave me new experiences when I replayed the old ones
embraced every part of me because they loved me
never judged me for not being linear
taught me to be tender to the body and soul they friend
encouraged me out of my shell
showed me the meaning of having a support system
showed me what it felt to have a family in strangers

New Experiences

I'm open to it all
open to new experiences at last
no longer feel like I'm cheating when I kiss someone new
when I lay alongside someone else

I'm open to it all
when someone else warms the sheets
we once were tangled under
I show them parts of my body he had once seen
kiss them with the tongue they once knew
wrap my hand behind their neck as they discover my body
only think of us in our embrace
look at them with the gleaming eyes that have forgotten
his face

I'm open to it all
I share secrets he once knew
tell them new things he'll never know about me
I don't hold him to the standard anymore
allow myself to meet new people
allow myself to experience new things he'll never hear of

Epilogue

This is where I'm at now. If you take any advice from this book let it be this final chapter.

Humanly Things

There's no shame in wanting love
humans are relational beings
we're meant to be in relationships
hold someone's hand when we're scared
cuddle next to someone when it gets cold
share our fears to someone we trust
talk about our day to a listening ear
want to spend our time with someone we love
it's okay to want love
it's okay to want a relationship
it's okay to fall in love easily
we're all just humans
and there's no shame in simply being human

Feel Everything

Don't let people tell you to get over things. Don't let time make you feel ashamed for still feeling. If one day you feel like lying in bed all day and have the privilege to do so, do it. I used to set out a timeline for when I should be over the heartbreak.

Time can be an enemy. I was only beating myself up. Emotions arise in the most interesting random times, and the worst thing you can do is cover them up.

So, feel everything. You'll be okay matter of fact, you'll be better than okay.

What I Wish I Had Done After The Breakup

Don't stalk your ex
block them the minute it ends
the minute it ends
the person you once knew no longer exists.
even if it ends on good terms
you'll eventually get hurt

Don't enter a one-sided competition with your ex
there's no "winning" after a breakup
just because they move on before you doesn't mean
they won
doesn't mean they healed
doesn't mean they're doing better

If they found someone else
don't compare yourself to that person
their relationship is none of your concern
whether he is the same or better
they are dealing with someone you've let go of
let that be their problem
and maybe it isn't
maybe they're right for each other
but it doesn't dismiss that he wasn't right for you
there's someone right for you out there
allow that person to come into your life

You Are Fucking Awesome

Allow yourself the time to heal
be kind to yourself
give yourself awards for the small victories
spend time with yourself
date yourself
pick up a new hobby
pick up habits that challenge your brain and body
just then you'll be reminded of how strong you really are

Journal
be unapologetic
whoever doesn't get it will leave and only the real will stay
unleash your power
embrace the new you
they're fucking awesome

Don't Let Something Good Pass You By

A love that is right and tender for you will come
just when you least expect it
they will come
they will make every past wound feel like a small prick
their love will feel like you're first real love
it will feel like coming up for fresh air
crispy air with vibrant colors to paint new horizons
you won't remembers past moments

It will just be them
they'll understand you in ways only real love can
they'll see you and accept you
they'll love everything you hate about yourself
they'll show you to be kind to yourself
the right love will come to you
the one that is catered and perfect for you
and there is no need to hold resentment because everything
happens for a reason
take past lessons as just that, lessons
lessons to prepare you for the right one
so when the right one comes
they don't get away

Be Loyal to Yourself

It's hard to let go of someone.

You try to convince yourself you'll find each other again. Make excuses to allow them back into your life. There's beauty in being that loyal, but you're being loyal to repeated pain.

The right one won't hurt you like that. Betray you, treat you like an enemy. They won't let you get away and find others, and reappear when they want you again. Would you do that to someone you love?

It's time to find someone that reciprocates the love you give them. Wouldn't that be sweet? To be shown the same love you give.

That exists.

You have to let go of the past and look ahead. Things end for a reason, and trust that there is someone else better for you. Allow that love to find you.

Please Be Kind to Yourself

Don't hate yourself for falling
don't blame yourself for choosing the wrong one
see the beauty of your heart
to allow itself to fall for someone and be so tender
to love so deeply and even if bruised choose to love again
don't let one error keep you from loving again
don't punish your heart
don't give that power to someone else
they don't get to keep your love
they don't deserve it
cherish your heart
that ever-so sensitive and loving organ

Don't Ruin Yourself for a Ruin

People are cruel
some have only been show cruelty so they deflect it onto
others
so many factors go into people treating you badly
the last thing you should do is convince yourself you
deserved it
kind people attract the most wounded people
but be selfish
don't pour your energy into people who lack being human
who don't recognize their actions
who don't feel remorse
don't ruin yourself for someone spreading you thin to glue
themselves together

Time Heals (Trust me it really does)

Very cliché
but time heals
I know it sometimes feels like your world is ending
that there's no purpose
that you'll always be stuck in that feeling
that you'll never feel anything for anyone again
you get clouded with every negative emotion in the book
and when it gets really bad, please go talk to someone
talking to a stranger who knows nothing
their professional perspective can calm down the storm in
your mind

And time heals
for some it goes quicker and for others it's a slower burn
but it burns
let time take its course and don't rush it
weeks, months, years
whatever it takes but you'll be okay
and when you look back, you'll smile
at the new memories you've made that you didn't realize you
were making

But live
don't let the past consume your precious time
don't miss out on the memories happening in front of
your eyes
don't betray yourself like that
enjoy and relish in the privilege that is now

breathe in the moments
dance through the pain
be here
be in the now
with time you'll get over it

Know that you are loved, and you'll get over it.

The End

Afterword

Thank you for making it through my whole journey. This book was in the works for around 2 years. I knew to make it genuine I had to capture my full experience of heartbreak. I wrote many of these poems especially in the beginning with tears streaming down my eyes. I didn't know at the time I wanted to create a book but writing poems about how I felt seemed to be the only thing getting me out the dark. It wasn't until I finally began healing that thoughts of a book came up. I remember how alone and insane I felt for feeling so deeply over a relationship that didn't last that long but affected me profoundly. So, I gathered up my poems and wrote new ones. I wrote this book as a reminder to myself and others that we're not alone. I channeled raw emotions in these poems, hoping that its authenticity can relate to others. I hope that some of these poems make people feel like someone else gets it.

At first the title was me telling my ex, "Hey, I wrote you a letter" and it contained all the things I never said to him. Although that title still stands it also became a letter to everyone reading. I see you and here is my poetic hug to you.